Who Was Joseph Stalin?
Biography Kids
Children's Historical Biographies

BABY PROFESSOR

EDUCATION KIDS

Speedy Publishing LLC
40 E. Main St. #1156
Newark, DE 19711
www.speedypublishing.com

Copyright 2017

All Rights reserved. No part of this book may be reproduced or used in any way or form or by any means whether electronic or mechanical, this means that you cannot record or photocopy any material ideas or tips that are provided in this book

Was Josef Stalin a hero or a monster? He helped his country win World War II, but while he was the leader of the Soviet Union, more than 20 million people died and millions more suffered because of his decisions. Let's learn about this complicated man.

Birth and Early Life

Josef Stalin was born in Georgia, in the Caucuses Mountains, in 1878. His name when he was born was Josef Vissarionovich Djugashvili. When he was in his thirties he changed his name to Stalin, which comes from the Russian for "man of steel".

His family was very poor, and his early life was hard. His father, a shoemaker, was a violent man when he was drunk, and he was often drunk. His mother worked washing clothes for other people. Josef was their only child. Stalin caught smallpox when he was seven years old. He did not die, but his face was badly scarred.

As a teenager, Stalin won a scholarship to study in the seminary in Tbilisi. He was supposed to be studying to become a priest, but secretly he was studying the thoughts of radical thinkers like Karl Marx. The seminary expelled him, saying he had missed too many exams. Stalin always said it was because his thoughts were too radical for the seminary and for the church.

Life Under the Czars

At that time, Russia was an empire. Its leader was the Czar, and the top of society were the imperial family with its many princes and princesses, and a huge number of counts and dukes. The very top of society had almost all political power and most of the wealth of the country. They identified their interests as those of the other royal families in Europe, with which they were related, and rejected any sort of move toward democracy.

The next layer was a growing class of merchants and business people. Their interests were to expand opportunities for business, no matter who was in charge. Below the merchants were the "kulaks". These were rural land-owners who controlled vast territories and the lives of the peasants, or serfs, who made up the bottom of society. Life for serfs was hard, because so much of the nation's resources went to support the upper class.

Russia when Stalin was born was very much a rural economy. There was not much industry, and the wealth of those in the cities depended very much on how well the harvests went in the country.

Radical Thoughts

Many people thought that the Russian system was little better than slavery. They felt that the nation's riches should benefit all of its citizens. The people who had the wealth and power wanted to hold onto it, and there were strikes and riots. Sometimes the army was called out to fight with protesting serfs and peasants.

Stalin was convinced the system had to change. He helped organize labor unions and took part in strikes and demonstrations. He joined Vladimir Lenin's Bolshevik Party, which wanted radical change in society. "Bolshevik" literally means "those in the majority", but very soon the word came to mean "violent trouble-makers".

Stalin was involved in crimes, including robbing banks, to get money to help the Bolshevik Party. He was arrested several times, and was sent into exile in Siberia, far away from all Russian cities.

Revolution and Government

In 1912, Lenin made Stalin part of the central committee of the Bolshevik Party. Stalin worked hard and gained power and influence.

In 1914, Russia went to war against Germany. The war did not go well, and people of all classes suffered. Lenin pushed for a new government that would take Russia out of the war. This attracted support from many people who did not worry about what else Lenin and his party might stand for.

In 1917, after a confused period, the Bolsheviks seized power and Lenin became the leader of Russia. In 1922, Russia was renamed the Soviet Union. Stalin was the General Secretary of the Bolshevik Party. He used this position to put his friends and supporters in key positions in the party.

The Bolshevik party eventually became the Communist Party. Anyone who wanted to advance in any career, even as a teacher, doctor, or scientist, had to belong to the party and agree with its teachings.

Stalin as Leader

Lenin died in 1924 and Stalin became head of the party and the government after a nasty struggle with several other party leaders.

Stalin felt that the Soviet Union had to change from being a country of peasant farmers to a land of industry and growth. He created several multi-year plans to develop industry and to join individual farms into collectives. This attacked the kulak land-holders, who resisted the takeover of their lands. Many were shot, and others were forced into exile. At the same time, a series of crop failures and resulting famine caused hardship across the whole country. Millions of people starved to death.

Knowing how he had risen to power himself, Stalin was fearful and suspicious of any possible rivals. He acted harshly to arrest rivals and destroy their power bases, and to break up any structure in the party and government that was not loyal to him. Stalin's "gulag" system of forced labor camps across Siberia held millions of political and economic prisoners, many arrested for little or no reason beyond that Stalin did not like them.

Writer Alexander Solzhenitsyn told a story of a community meeting. The chairman started the meeting with a round of applause for Comrade Stalin. The applause went on and on, and finally the chairman stopped applauding and sat down so the meeting could start, and everyone else stopped applauding as soon as he did. The next day the chairman was arrested and sent to the gulag. The arresting officer told him, according to Solzhenitsyn, "Don't ever be the first person to stop clapping."

By the end of the 1930s the Soviet Union was becoming a major industrial power, but at the cost of liberty and even life for millions of its citizens.

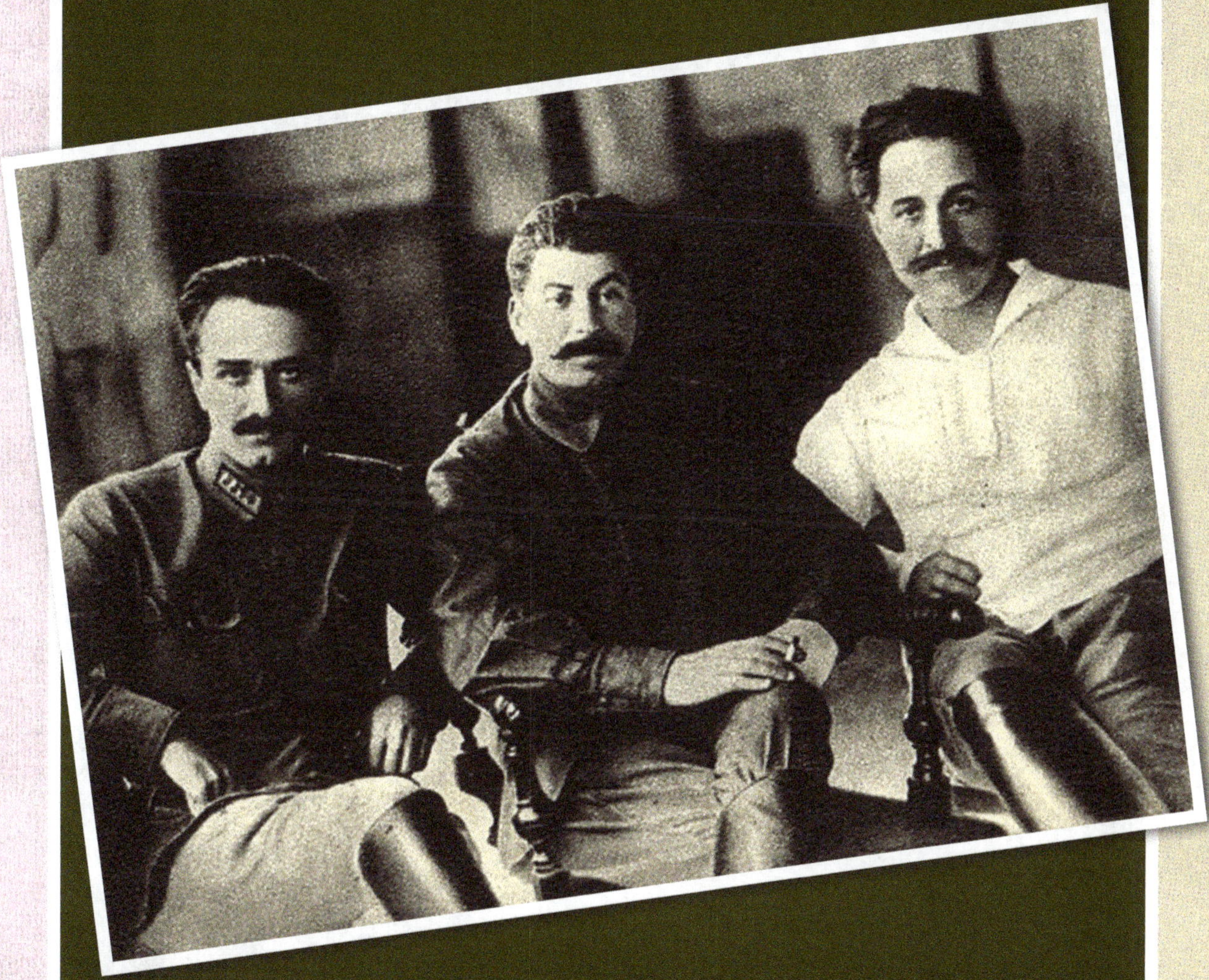

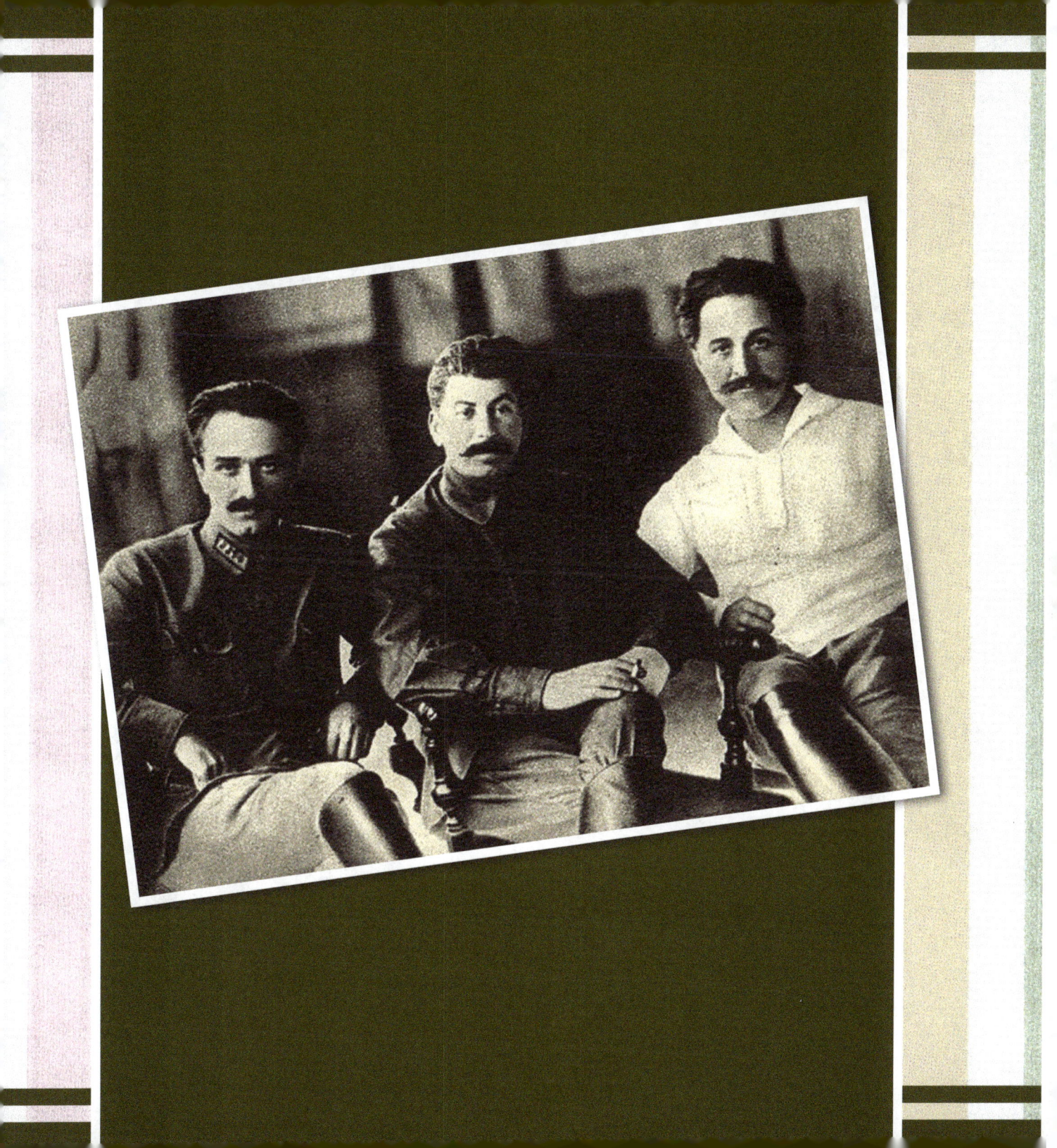

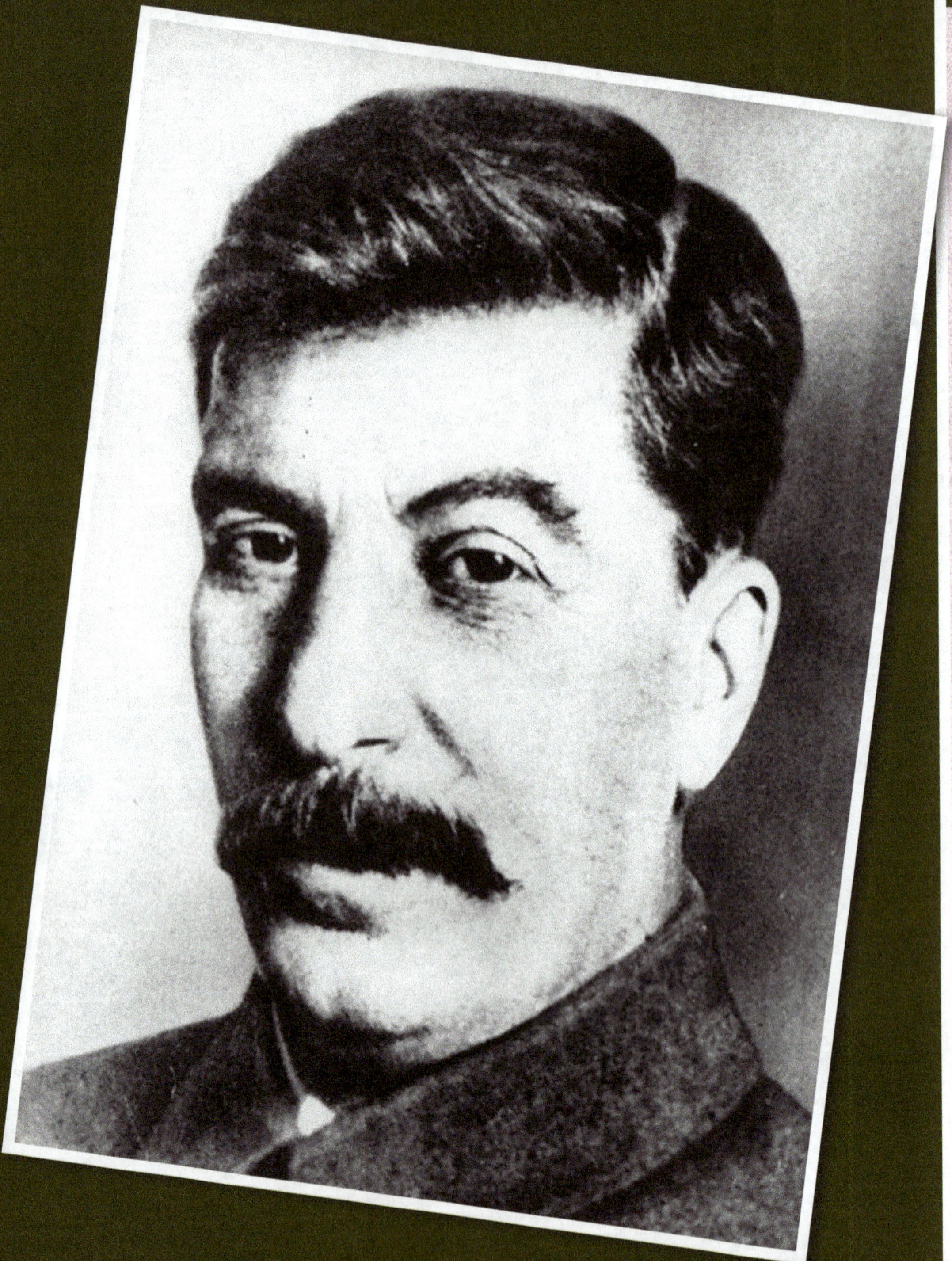

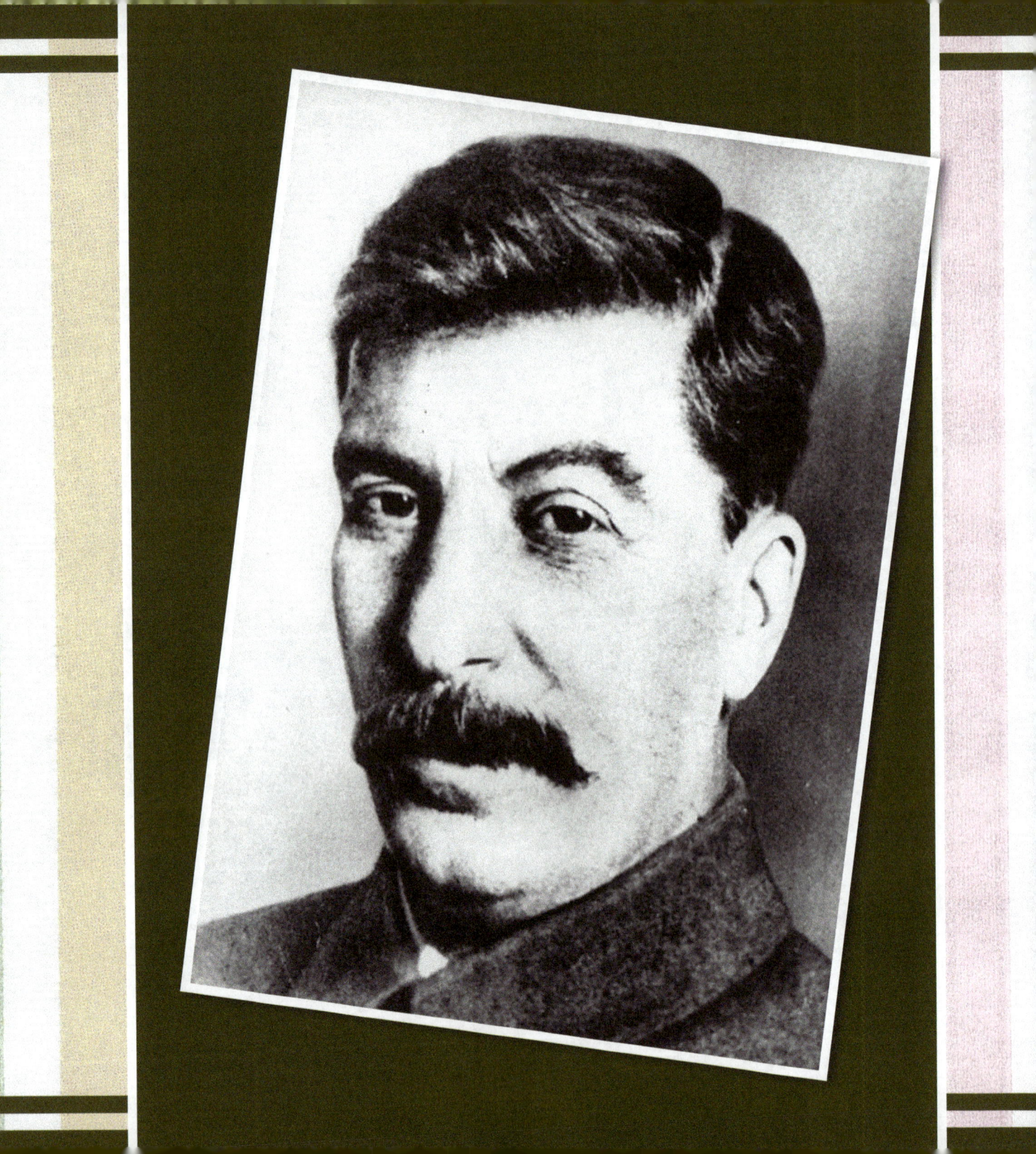

Stalin in World War II

As the world moved toward war in the late 1930s, Stalin signed a treaty with Adolf Hitler of Germany. Stalin's goal was to gain territory and influence while avoiding war with a strong enemy.

At the start of World War II, in 1939, Germany and the Soviet Union combined to divide up Poland. But in 1941 Germany violated the treaty and launched a massive attack against the Soviet Union. The United States and Great Britain had tried to warn Stalin that the attack was coming, but he did not believe them. He ignored his own intelligence services, too, so Russia was unprepared for the German attack.

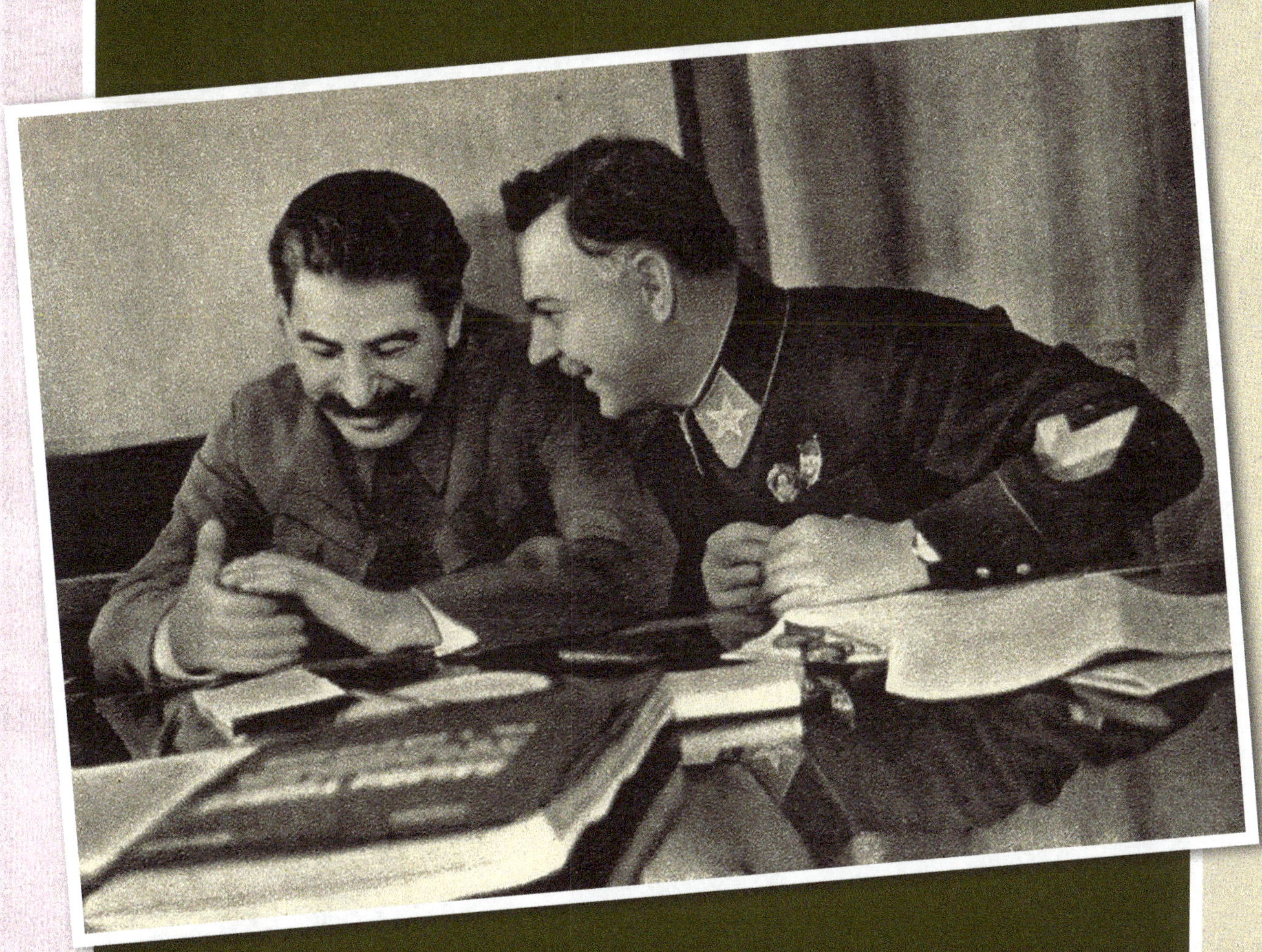

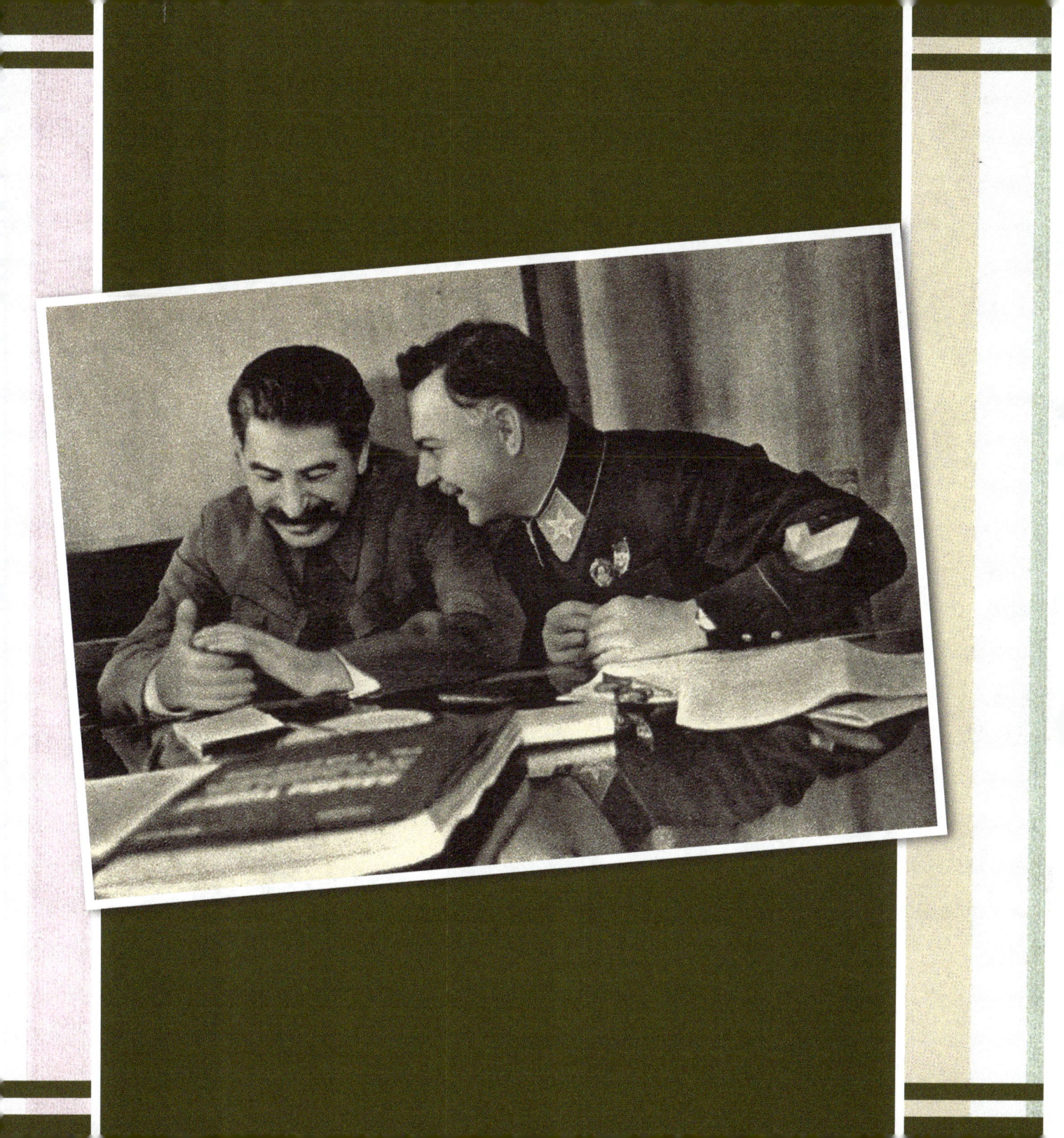

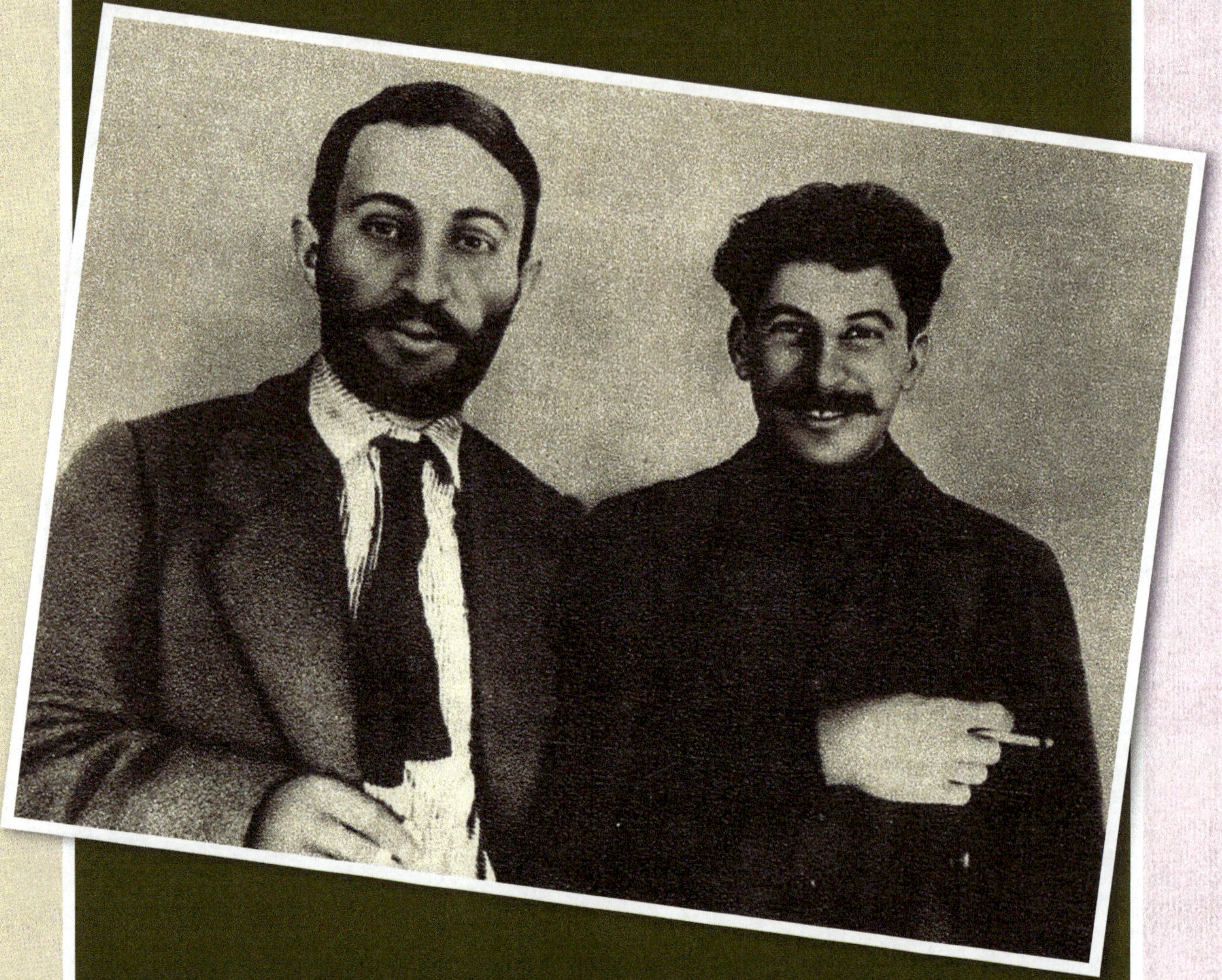

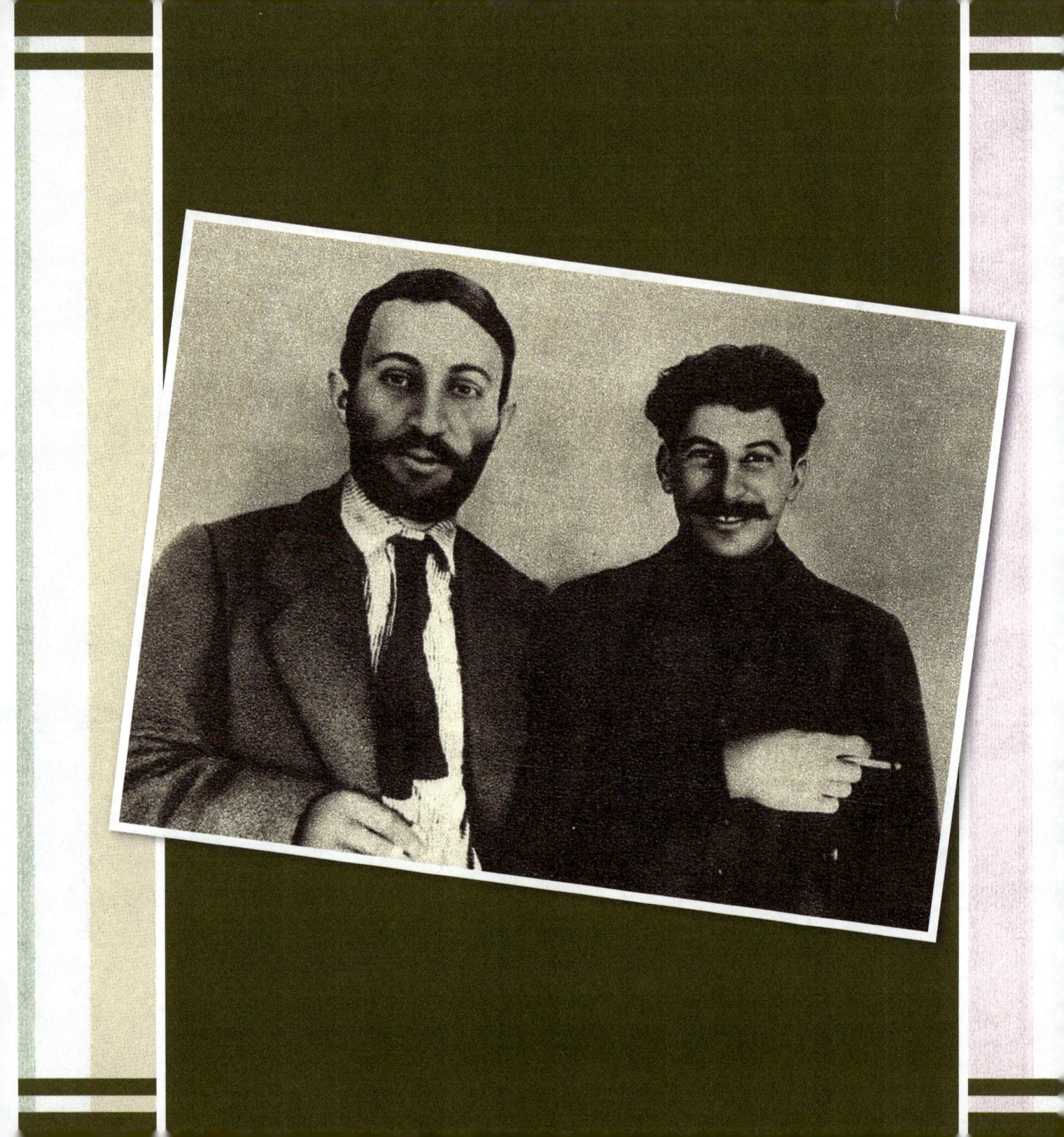

The Germans fought almost all the way to Moscow before the Soviet armies could slow their advance. The tide turned when the Germans lost the battle of Stalingrad and had to start retreating. The Soviet Union ended up on the winning side, but at the cost of over 20 million deaths in the war.

The Cold War

Stalin realized his dream of expansion for the Soviet Union after World War II. All the countries of Eastern Europe fell under Soviet influence or direct control. The Soviet Union developed its own atomic bomb, so it could match the power of the United States. Stalin encouraged adventures by minor countries such as North Korea, to which he gave permission to attack South Korea in 1950.

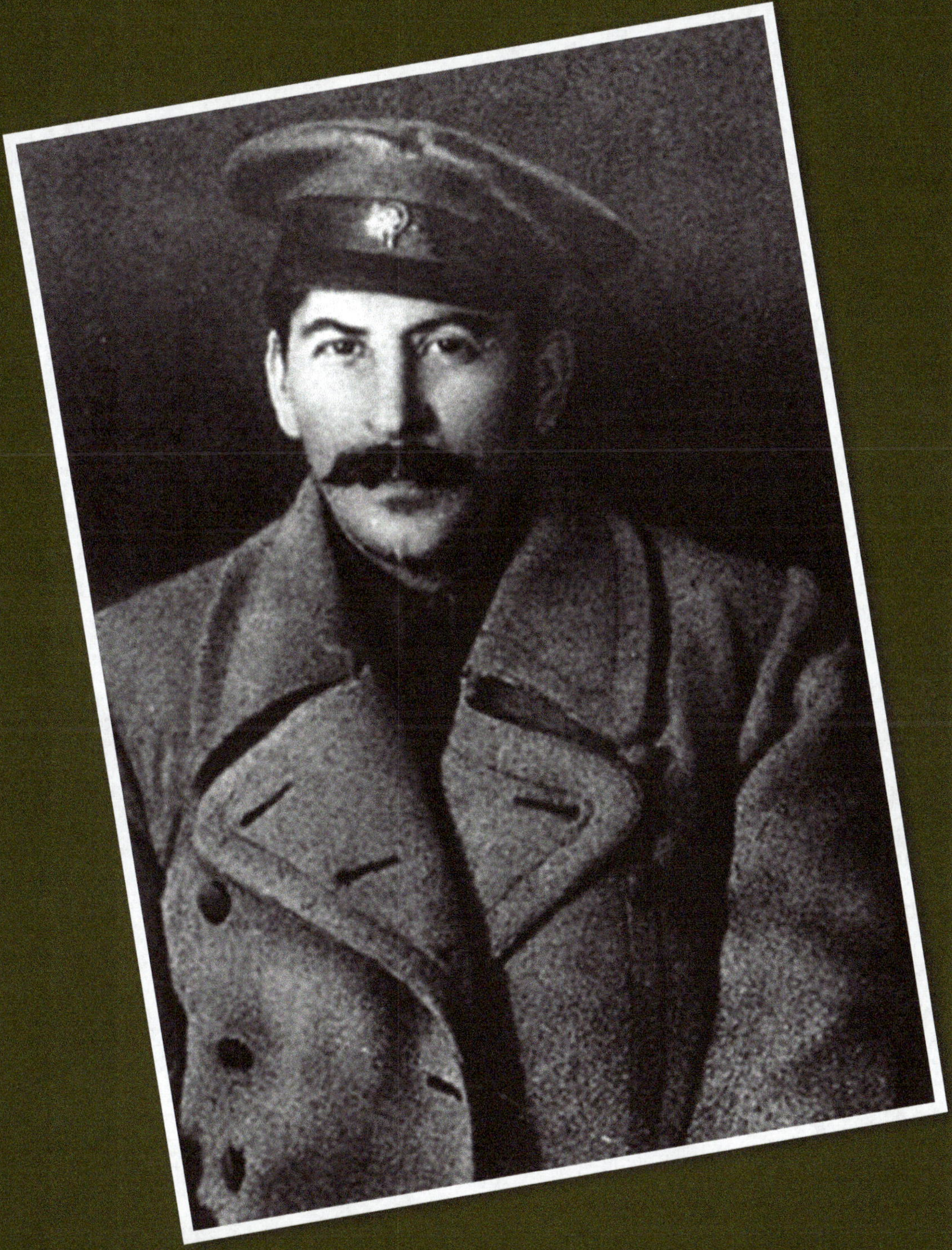

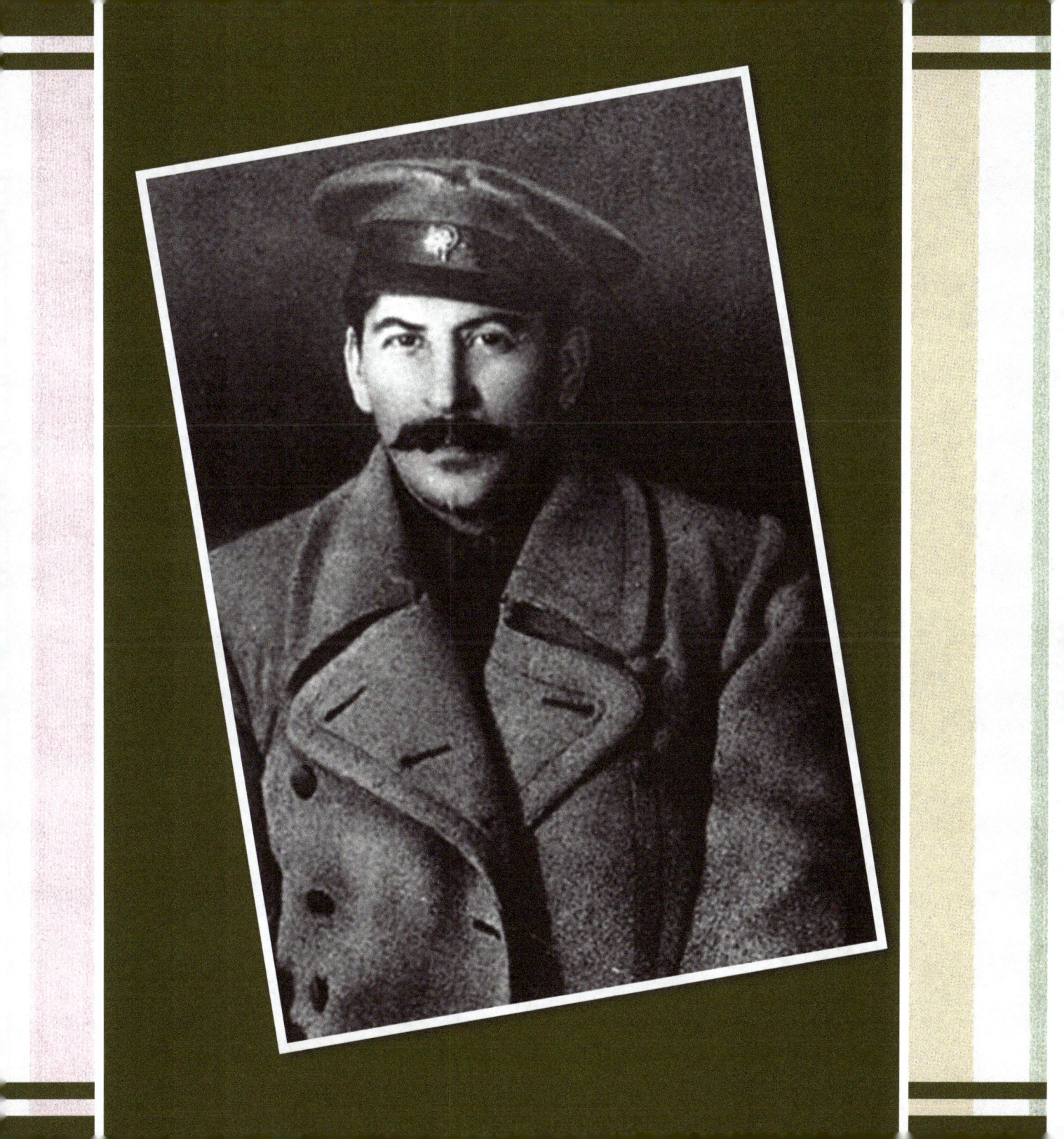

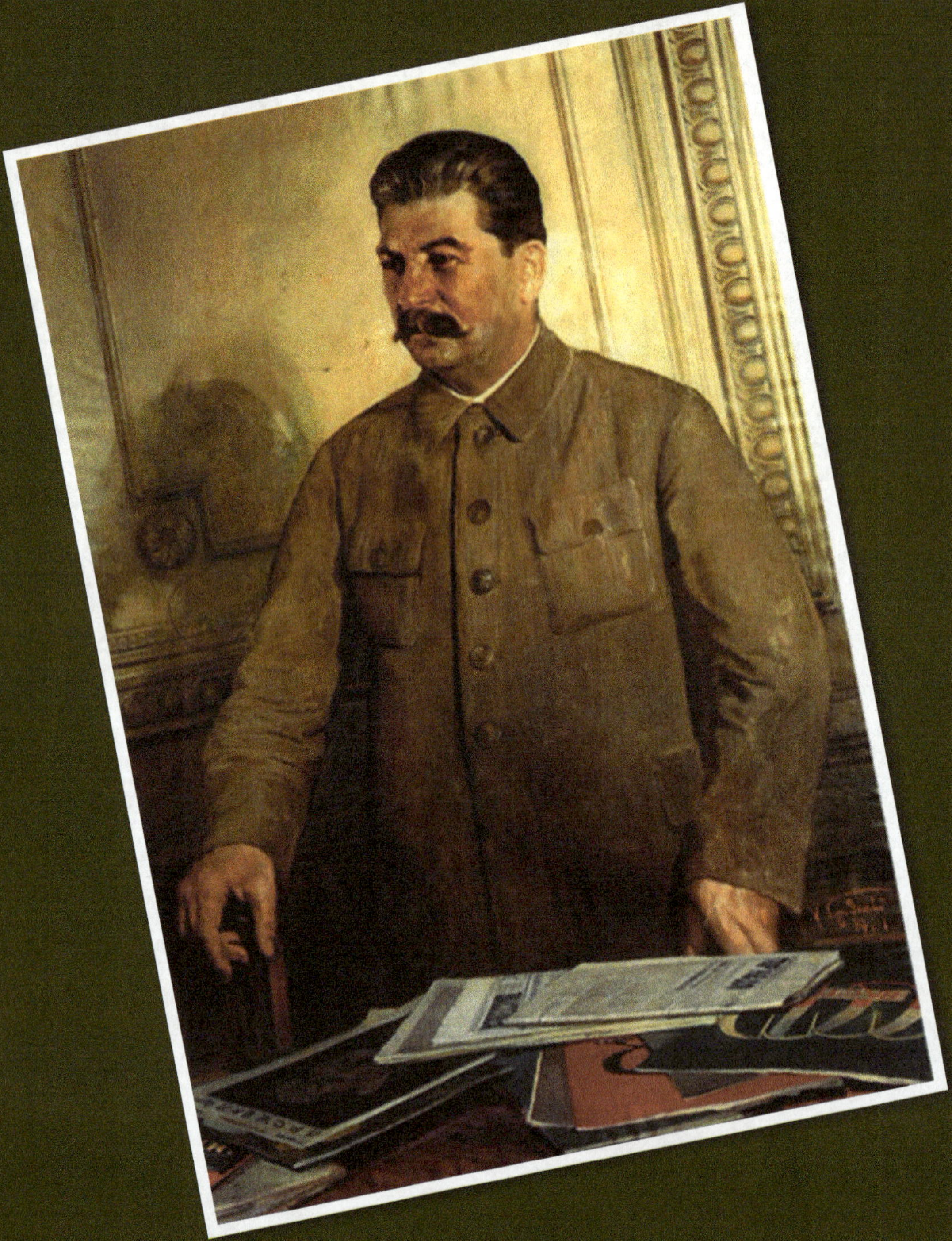

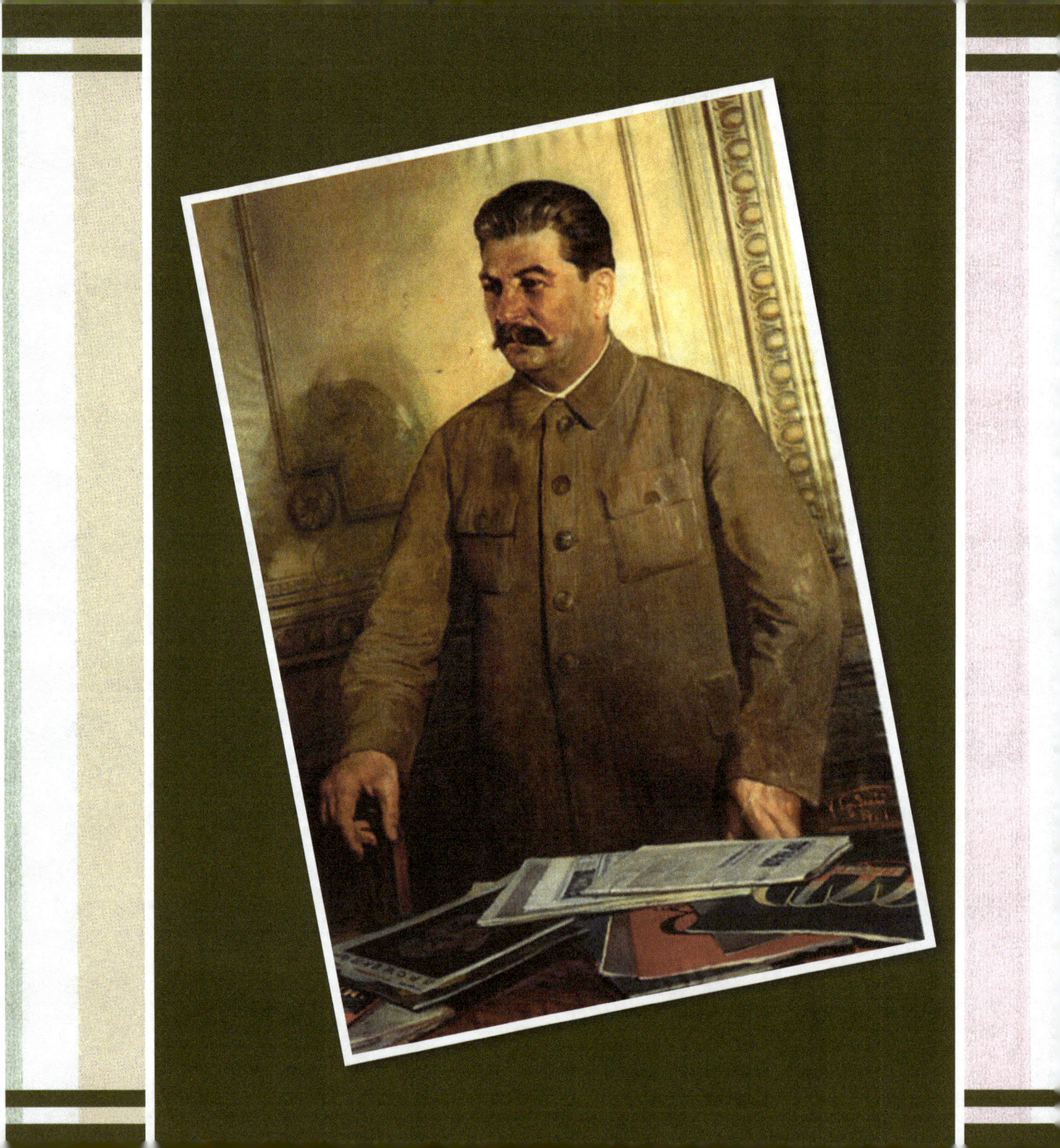

At the same time, Stalin increased the cult of personality around himself. His name became part of the national anthem. People named cities, streets, squares, and schools after him. He persecuted anyone who seemed to disagree with him or to pose a threat to his power. Through the party, Stalin controlled the news media, television and radio broadcasts, and the theater. Artists tried to present Stalin as a strong leader in war, and "Uncle Joe" in times of peace.

During this time, those who were able to stay on Stalin's good side became rich and powerful, while anyone who made a challenging mistake might go from a position of power to a jail cell within a day.

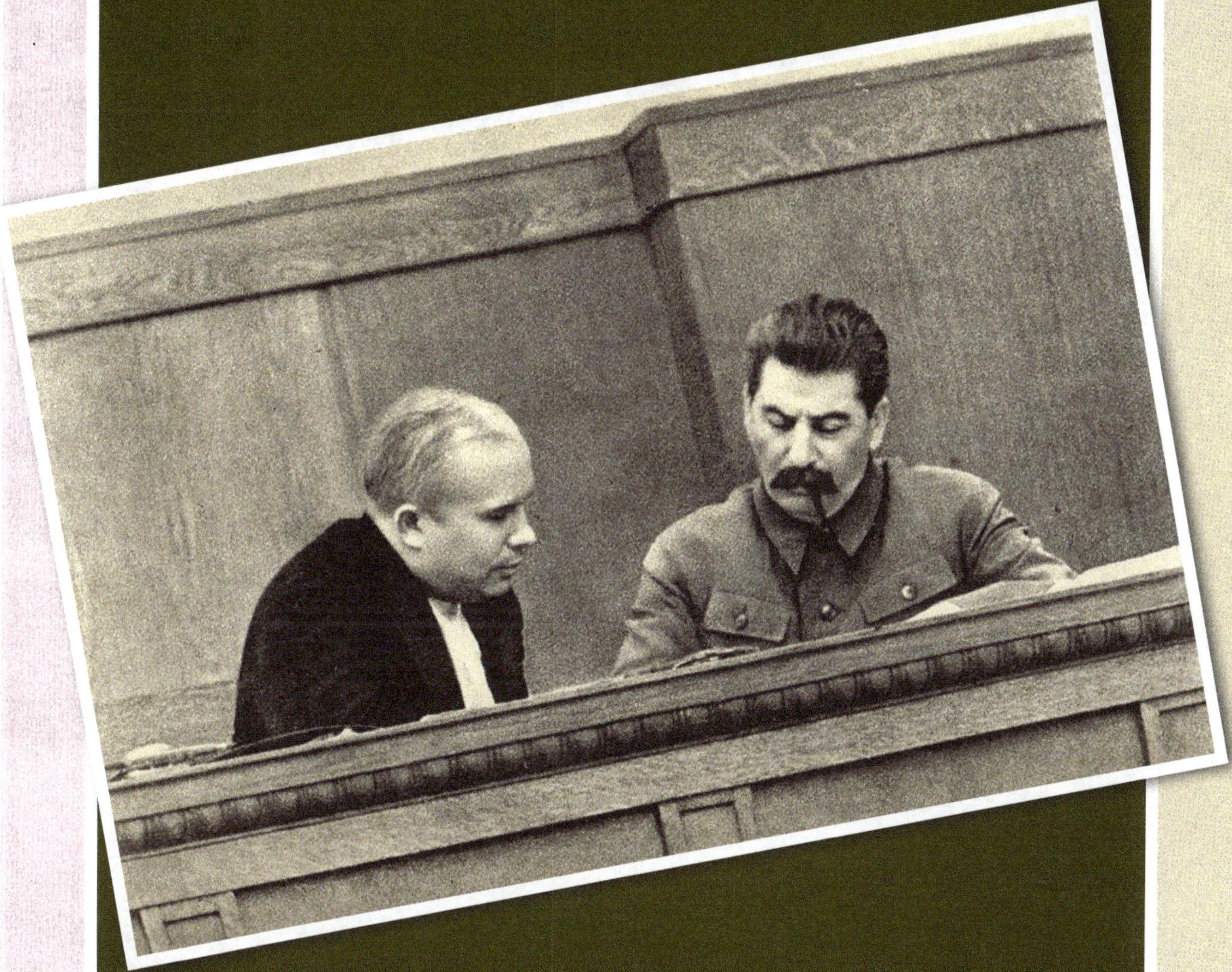

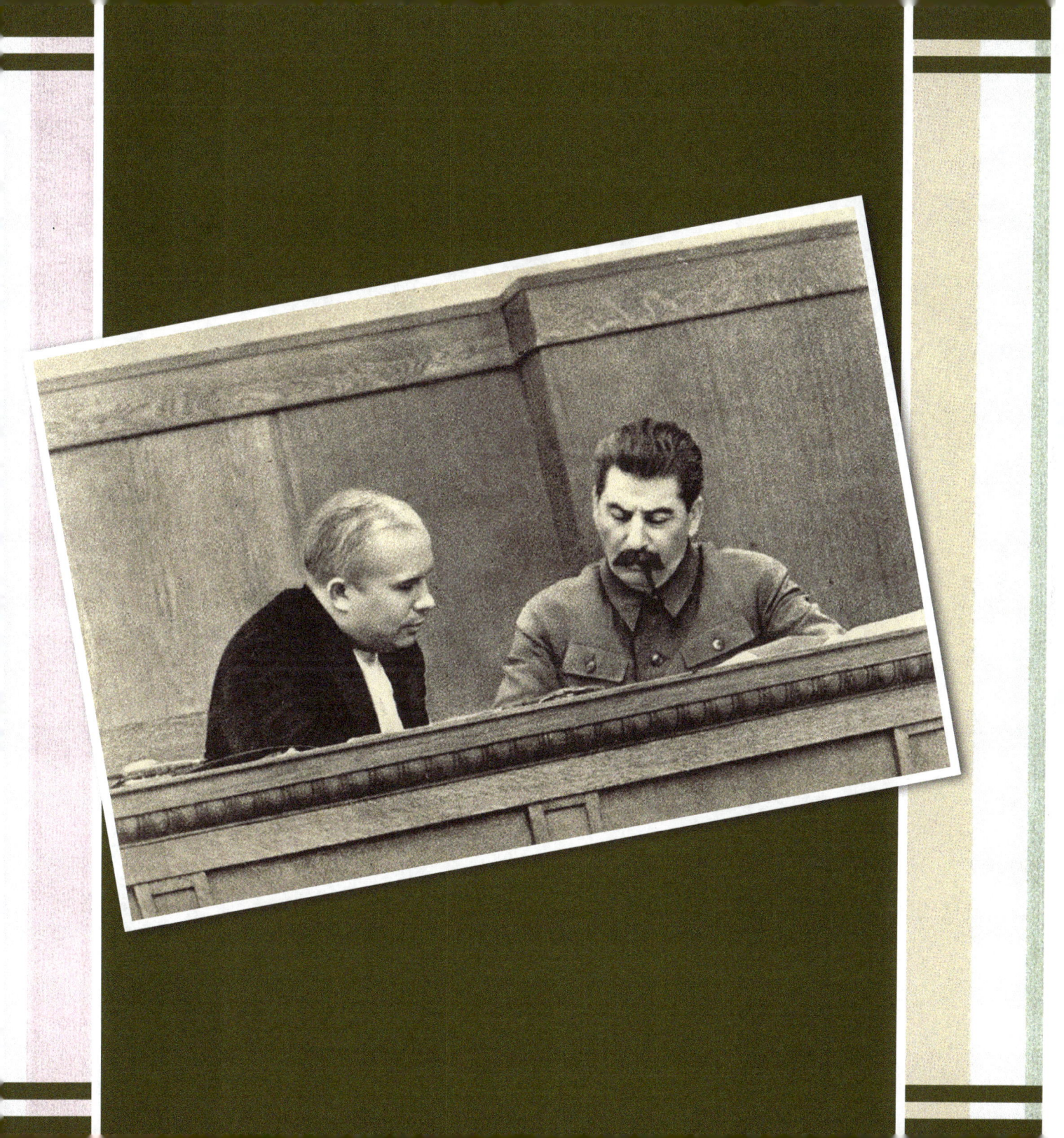

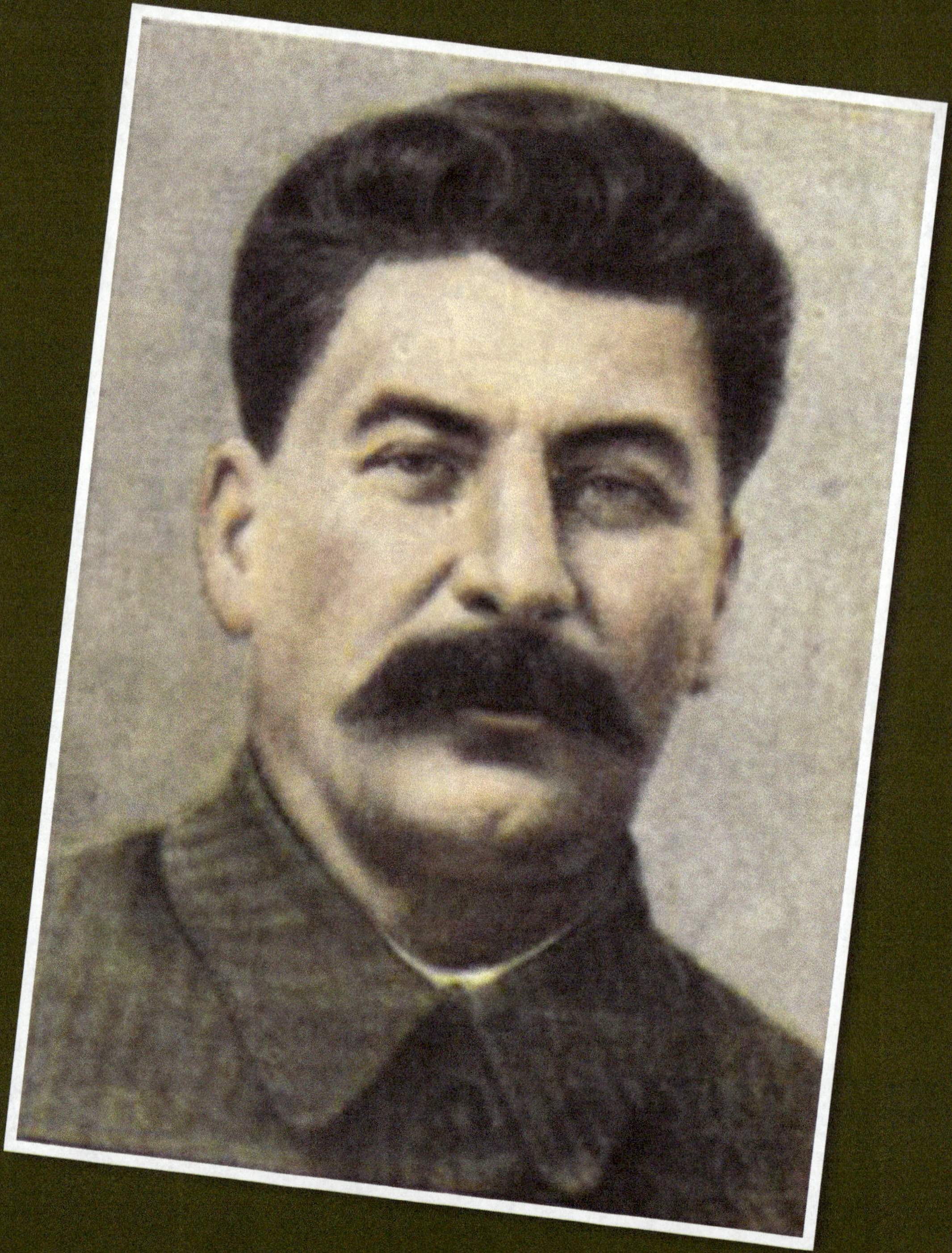

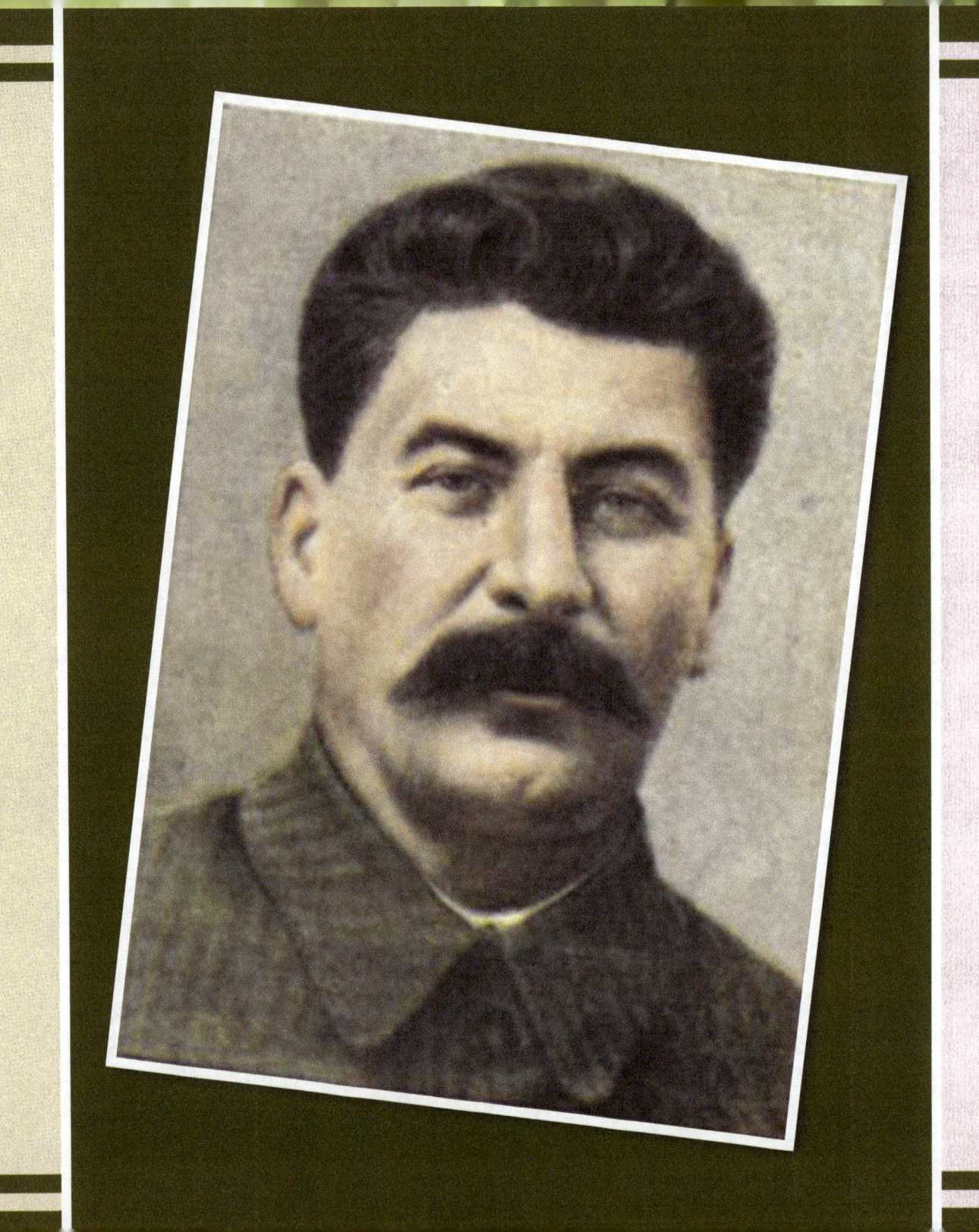

The Death of Stalin

Stalin's health became less and less good as he got older, and even with all the skill of the nation's doctors he could not be kept healthy forever. He suffered a stroke and died in 1953, at the age of 74.

Stalin's body was embalmed and placed beside the preserved body of Vladimir Lenin in a tomb in Red Square. A few years later his body was removed and buried nearby.

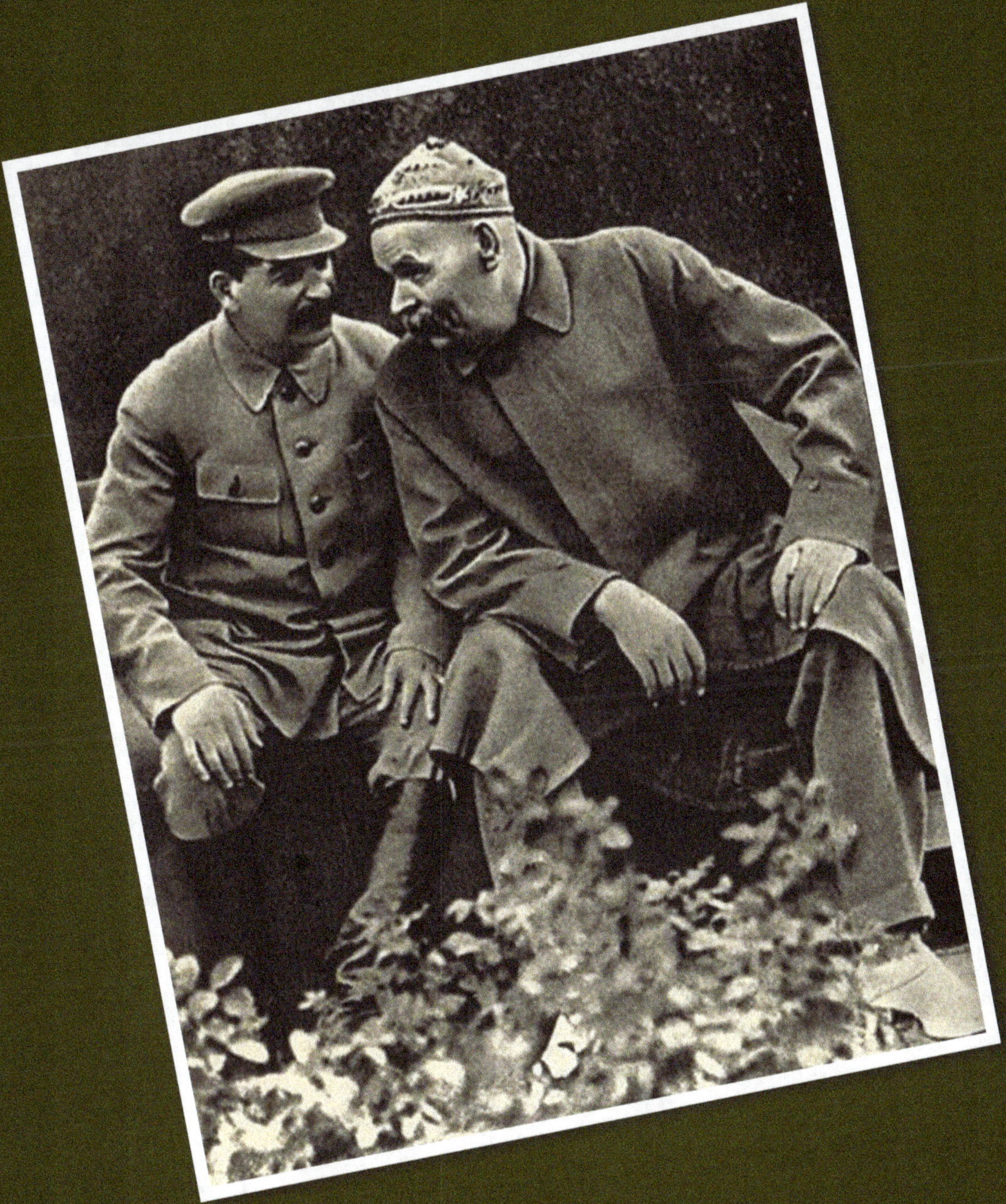

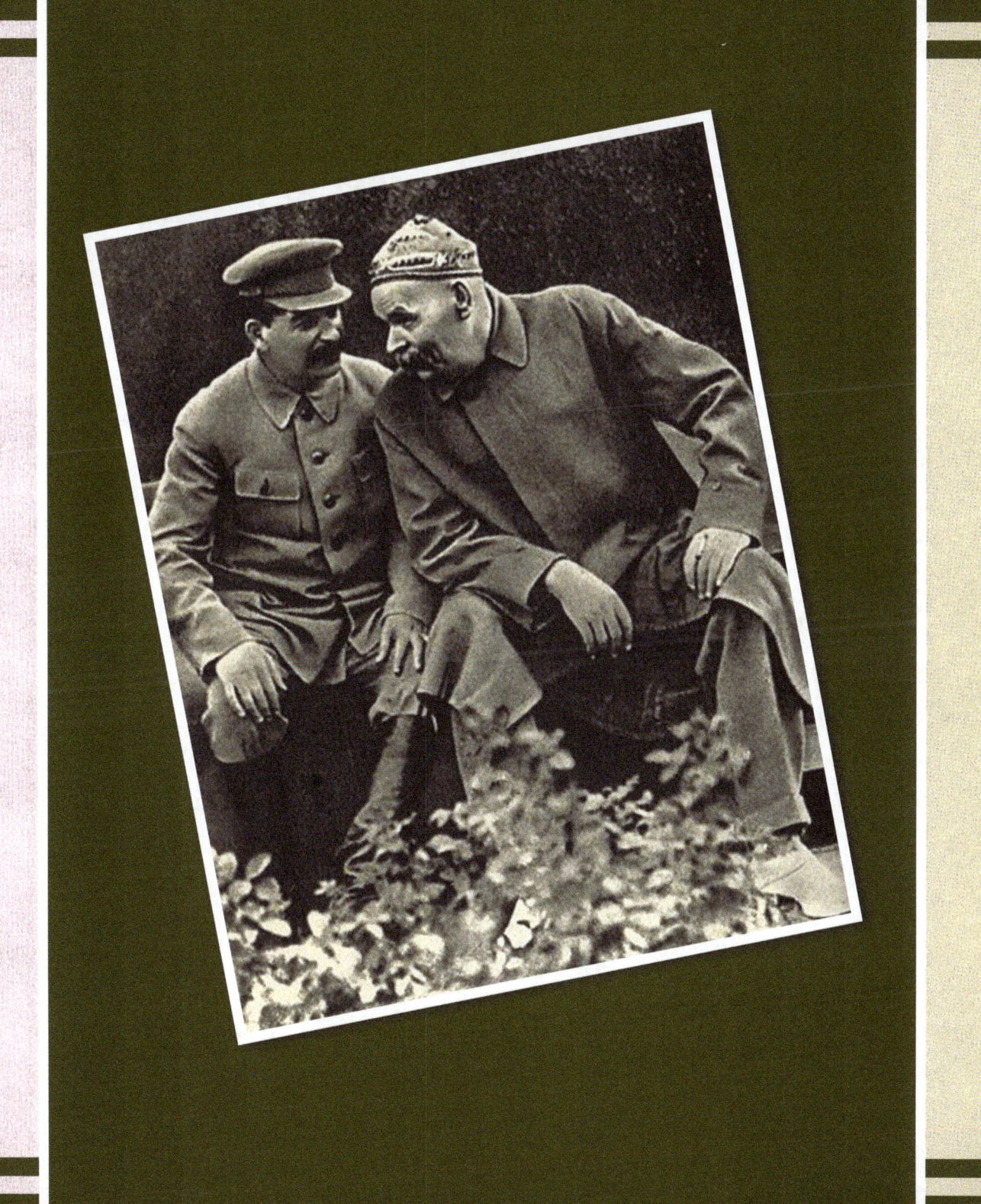

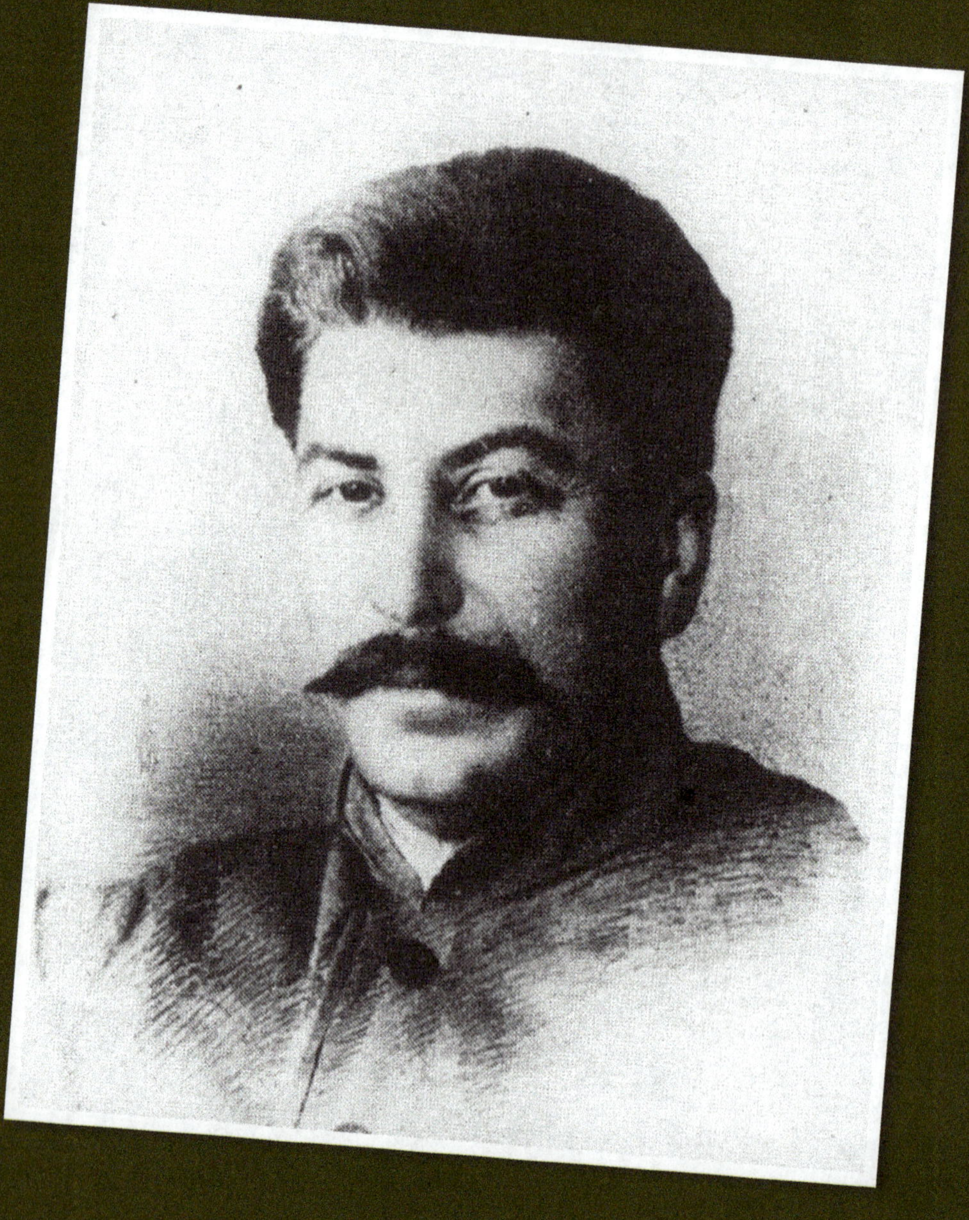

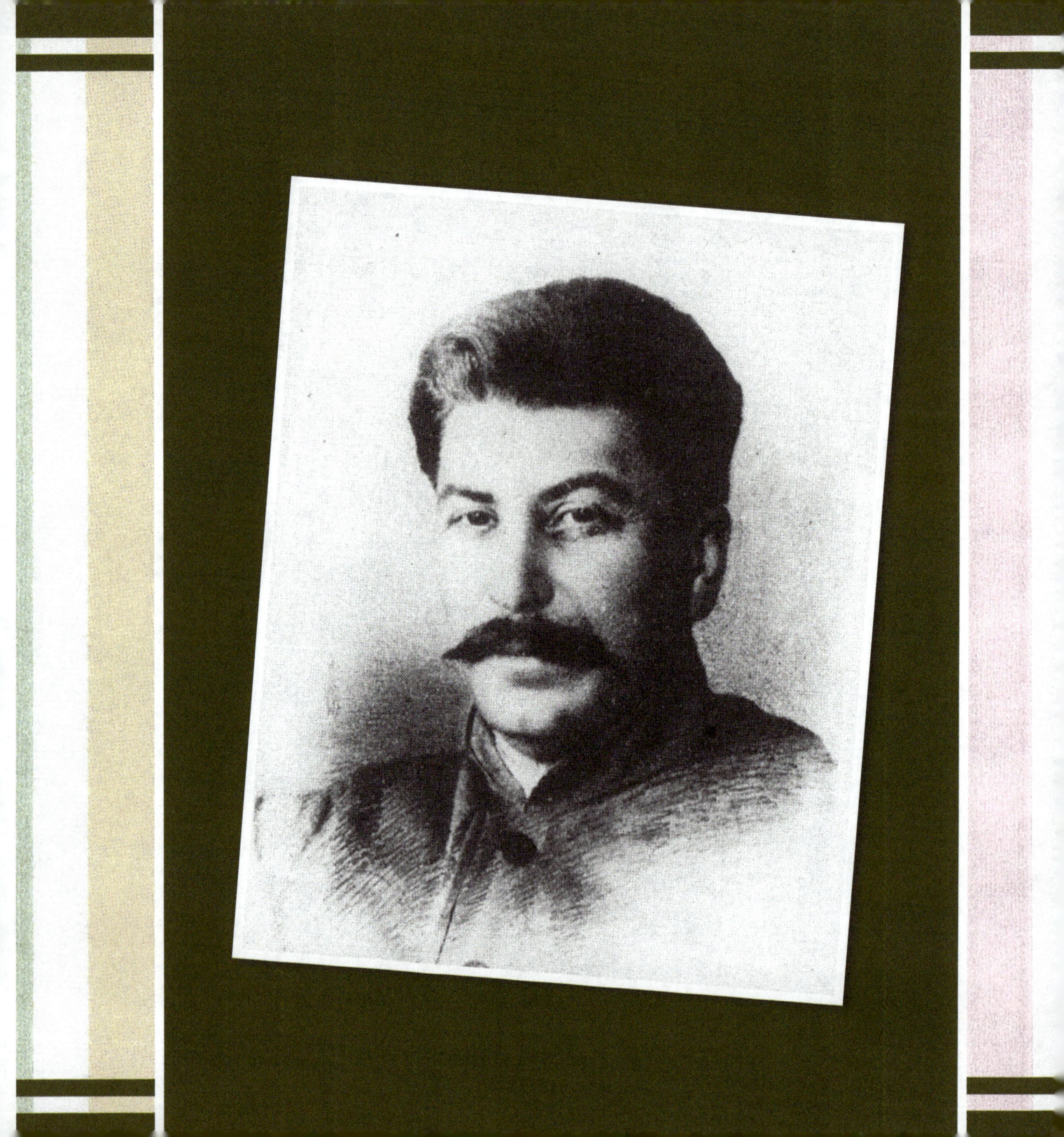

By his death, Stalin had moved his country from an agricultural economy to being a major economic power and industrial power, brought it through a world war to victory, and made the Soviet Union one of the great political forces in the world. On the other hand, you could say that nothing had changed at all politically: the country still had one powerful and ruthless person at its head, just as it had had under the Czars.

Stalin's policies probably cost the lives of over 20 million people, on top of those lost to famine and war while he was leader.

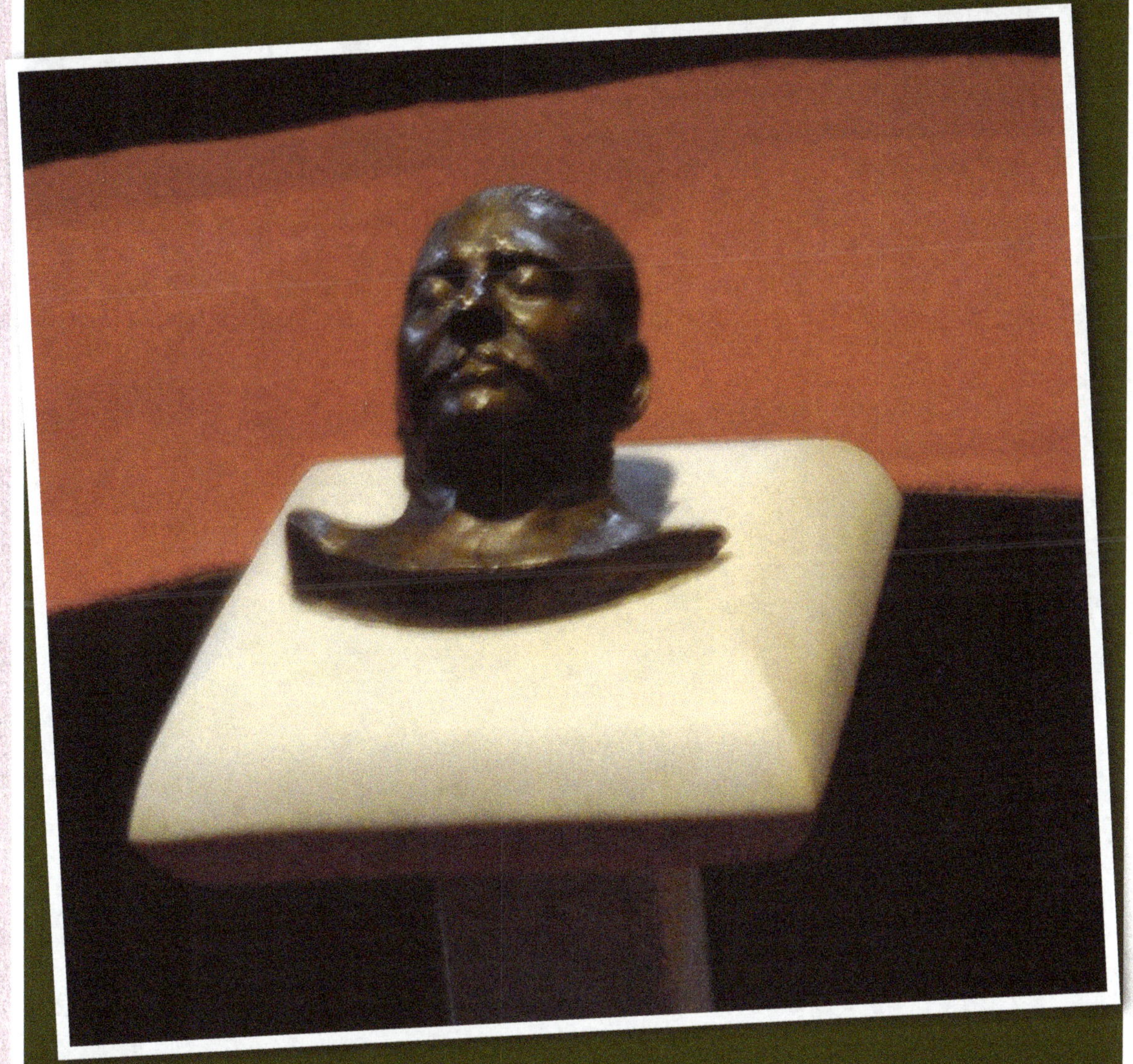

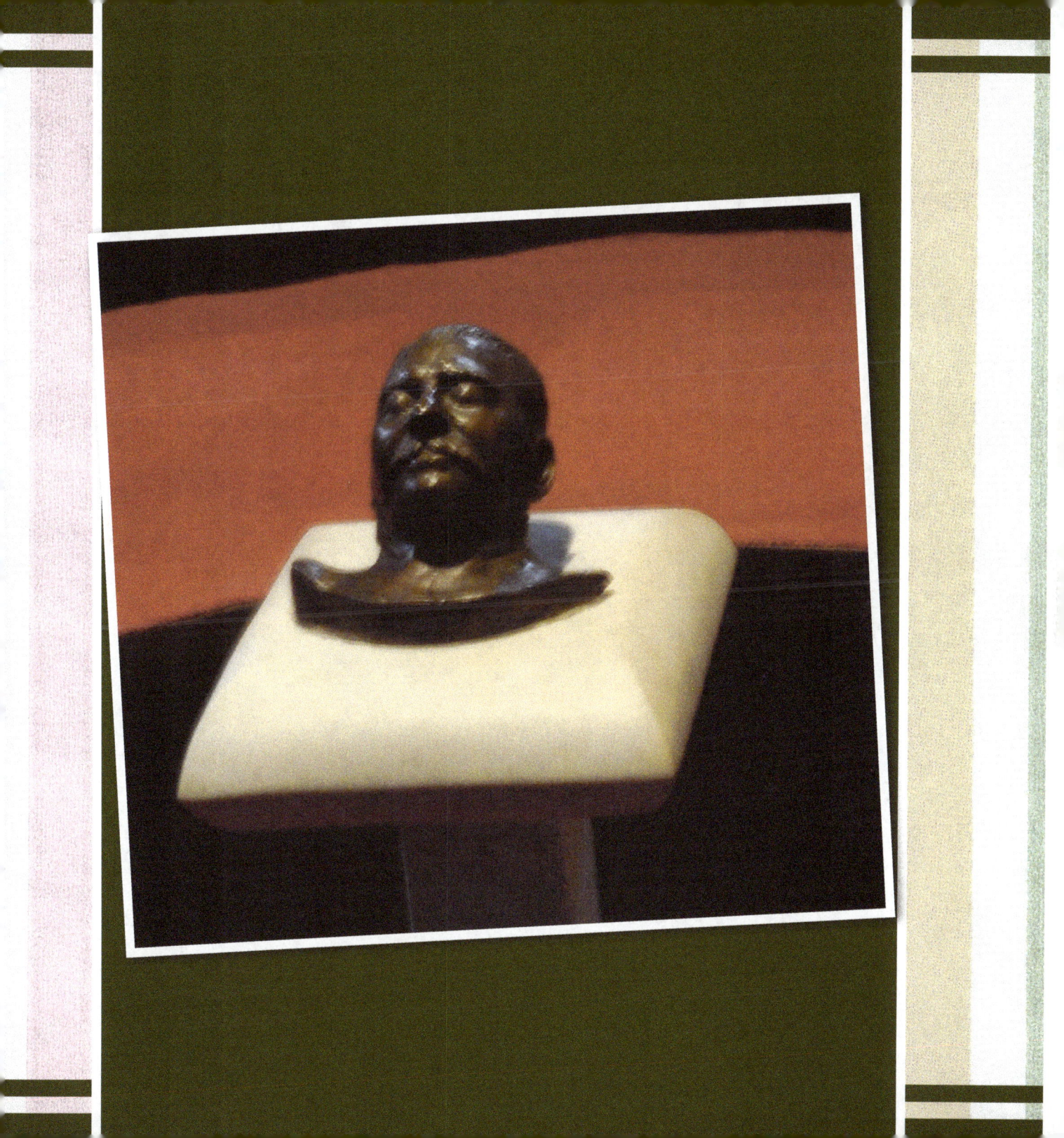

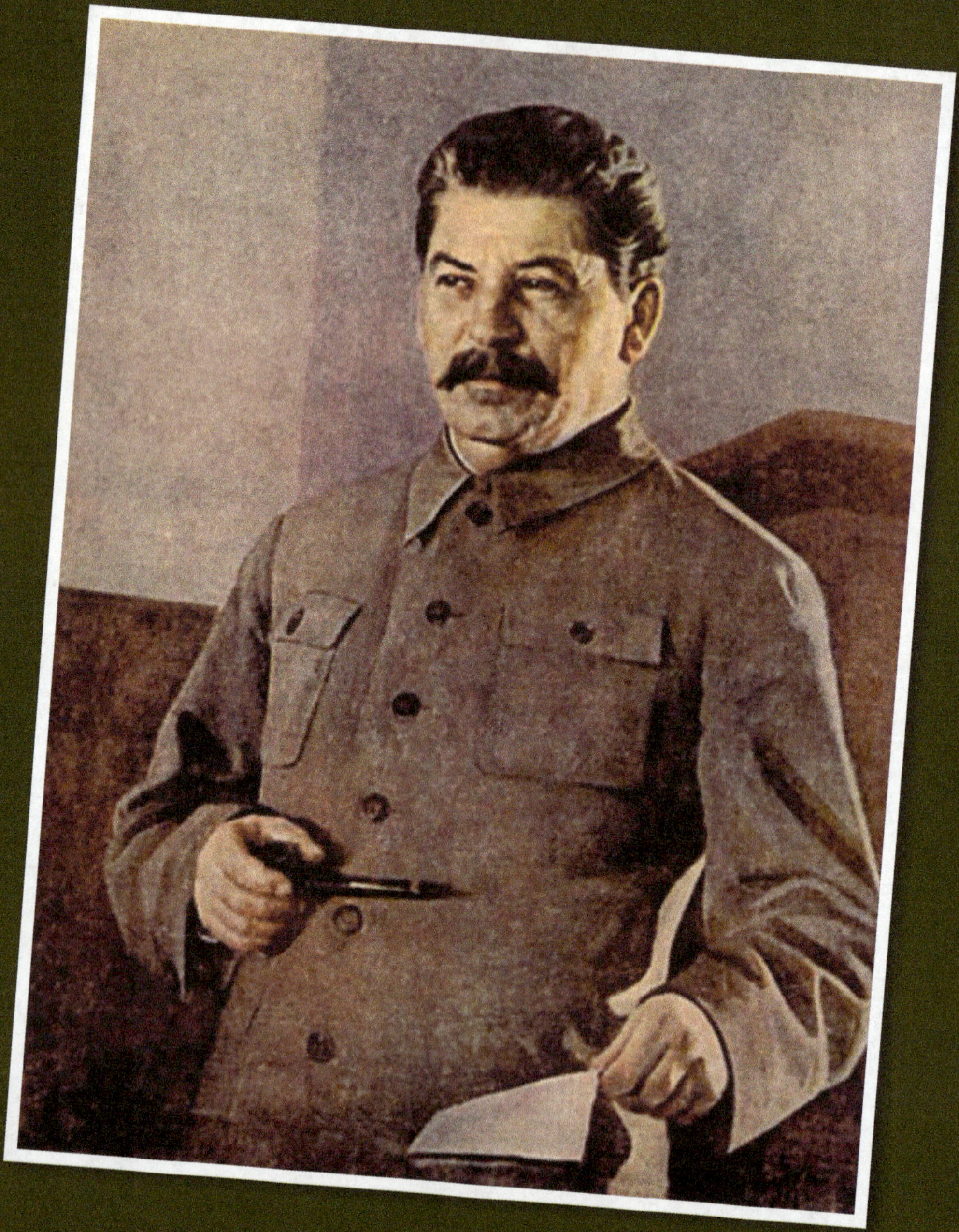

Leaders, Heroes, and Villains

People are very complicated. The best people have bad parts, and even the worst people have done some good. Read other Baby Professor books to learn about other leaders, heroes, and villains.

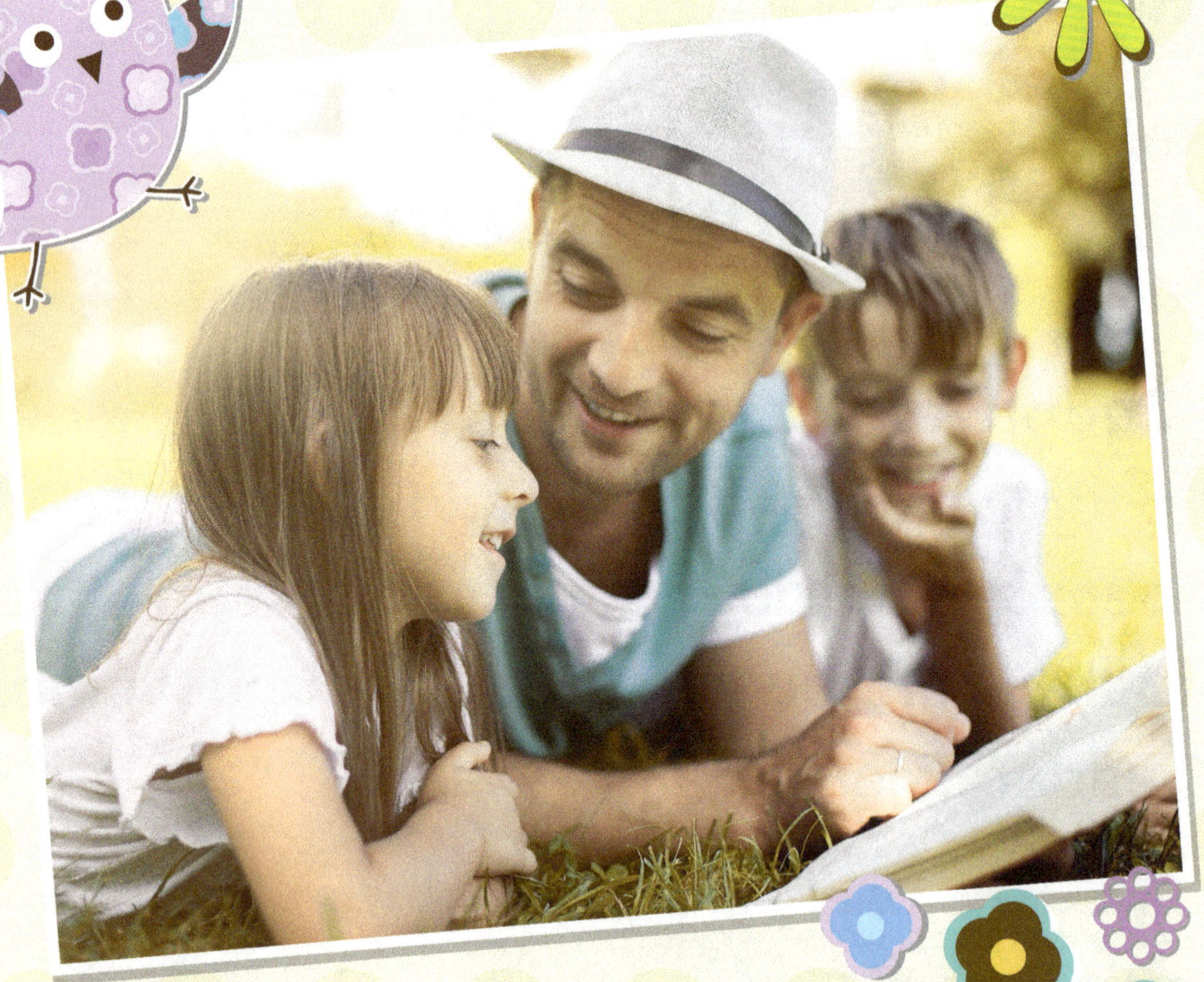

Visit

BABY PROFESSOR
EDUCATION KIDS

www.BabyProfessorBooks.com

to download Free Baby Professor eBooks and view our catalog of new and exciting Children's Books

CPSIA information can be obtained
at www.ICGtesting.com
Printed in the USA
BVHW091228170219
540465BV00005BA/180/P